The Ultimate Motorcycles

DIRT BIKES

Lori Kinstad Pupeza
ABDO Publishing Company

visit us at
www.abdopub.com

Published by Abdo Publishing Company 4940 Viking Drive, Edina, Minnesota 55435.
Copyright © 1998 by Abdo Consulting Group, Inc. International copyrights reserved in all
countries. No part of this book may be reproduced in any form without written permission
from the publisher.

Printed in the United States.

Photo credits: Allsport, Duomo, Peter Arnold, Inc., Sportschrome, Yamaha

Edited by Kal Gronvall

Library of Congress Cataloging-in-Publication Data

Pupeza, Lori Kinstad
    Dirt bikes / Lori Kinstad Pupeza.
        p.   cm. -- (The ultimate motorcycle series)
    Includes index.
    Summary: Discusses the history, riding, and racing of dirt bikes, including such aspects as
the engine, other parts, gear, and safety tips.
    ISBN 1-57765-001-8
    1. Trail bikes--Juvenile literature.   2. Motorcycling--Juvenile literature [1.Trail bikes. 2.
Motorcycling] I. Title. II. Series: Pupeza, Lori Kinstad. Ultimate motorcycle series
    TL441.P86 1998
    629.227'5--dc21

                                                          97-53100
                                                           CIP

Second printing 2002   AC

Warning: The series *The Ultimate Motorcycles* is intended as entertainment for
children. These activities should never be attempted without training, instruction,
supervision, and proper equipment.

Contents

Where They Ride

The most enjoyable part of riding a dirt bike comes from seeing the places it will take you. Most motorcycles can only be driven on paved roads. But bikers ride dirt bikes—sometimes called trail bikes—through forests and dirt trails. They can cruise over rocks and jump over obstacles.

Dirt bikes are made for the adventurous person who wants to see more than just a highway. Whether it's muddy trails or sandy back roads, a dirt bike can ride through it all. Designed for taking a beating, riders can drive dirt bikes through almost any condition. Sometimes a rider's biggest challenge is just staying on the bike.

Off-road riding can mean many things. It can mean riding for fun, competition, or even work. Lots of motorcyclists enjoy riding off the busy highways and onto dirt trails that ramble through the countryside.

Many people, young and old, are serious competitors and spend lots of time and money perfecting their skills on their dirt bikes. Others spend all day on dirt bikes for their jobs. Some cowboys have now replaced their horses with dirt bikes, as have the Royal Canadian Mounted Police. Even forest rangers now patrol the parks on trail bikes.

Some places in the country are too dangerous or too hard to get to on foot. Dirt bikes help workers get to electrical lines or telephone equipment that can't be reached with a four-wheeled vehicle. Dirt bikes aren't just for sport anymore.

A dirt bike can go almost anywhere.

History

The original sport of "scrambling" started in Britain in the 1920s. Scrambling means driving across fields, muddy paths, under tree branches, down rocky ravines, and through sandy lands. Avid cyclists drove some of the first motorcycles built over rough terrain just to test the machine's strength and endurance.

In 1899, an English motorcycle builder named E.J. Pennington advertised his motorcycle as being capable of "cross-country work." At that time, most motorcycle companies were trying to create a civilized image of motorcycling, calling their motorcycles "suitable for ladies." Mr. Pennington had other ideas.

Pennington's printed advertisement showed a man on a motorcycle flying over a river. Spectators were cheering and waving as the motorcyclist flew over two shocked people in a canoe. Today, off-road racing still captures the same excitement and awe that was in Pennington's advertisement.

Opposite page: Dirt biking has been a popular sport since the first dirt bike was introduced in 1899.

Types of Races

Over time, people started forming organized, official off-road races. These races are called off-road because the motorcycles stay off paved roads. Motocross, supercross, trials, and enduro racing are four different kinds of off-road races. They've become very popular in countries all over the world and all kinds of people enjoy them. All four of these races push the bike and its driver's skills to the limit.

Motocross racers drive on a hilly track filled with bumps and sharp turns. Most of the surface is hard to drive on. At the starting line, the drivers line up and hope to jump ahead of the rest of the pack before the course narrows. On the hills, motocross drivers do high-flying jumps.

There are different racing classes, determined by the engine size and the age of the riders. The outdoor track is in the shape of a winding circle, usually around one mile (1.6 km) long. The race lasts for a set amount of time. For example, each class might run two 20-minute races. Your place in each race is used to decide how you place overall. Racers can reach speeds up to 70 mph (112 kmph), but usually average 35 mph (56 kmph).

Supercross races are held in stadiums. An artificial race track is built with sand and dirt. This way spectators can watch without

having to walk through woods and climb muddy hills. They can sit in comfort and watch the action right from their seats. Supercross races aren't as challenging as motocross races because they are indoors, away from rain and cold. Trees and mountains aren't blocking the spectators' view.

Supercross racing is a good warm-up race for the more challenging motocross racing. The rules for supercross racing are similar to motocross racing. Supercross racers can show off their daring stunts to a cheering crowd in a stadium. Racers will do jumps and fly up to 70 feet (21 m) in the air!

Enduro racing entails a lot more stamina, both from the bike and from its rider. Enduro races can last up to 24 hours. To win, a

A motocross race is held outdoors on a winding circular track.

team of riders has to cover the farthest distance in a certain amount of time. The more sturdy the bike, the less time spent on repairs or tire changes. Every minute counts. The rider needs to be very good at identifying conditions that are ahead. He or she must know every trick of getting across nature's obstacles. The racer has to maintain a good clip, and at the same time know when to go slowly, and when to use speed. It is an exhausting sport reserved for only the best.

Trials began with motorcycle companies doing "trial" runs with their new models. Today, trials have been changed into a high-class test to push high-tech machines to their limits. Watching trials is a good way to become acquainted with the techniques of off-road riding. Trials competition requires riders to ride very slowly through a rough course without putting a foot down or stopping. The most skilled riders compete in trials.

More so than motocross and enduro racing, this sport requires a lot of balance and agility. With the other races, speed is essential, and stopping or walking your bike is allowed. In trials, the driver has to control the bike without letting it fall. Mastering off-road skills and techniques to conquer obstacles is key. Because driving a motorcycle at slow speeds is much harder than going fast, trials is especially tough. If you're serious about competing in any of these races, trials is the place to start.

Supercross races are held in stadiums on man-made dirt tracks.

The Motorcycle

Much can be learned about off-road racing just by looking at the bike. Dirt bikes need to carry riders over rough terrain with as much comfort and ease as possible. Although there are more similarities than differences among dirt bikes, the differences are important.

Dirt bikes are designed according to the specific activities in which they will be used. So, what makes a good dirt bike? Most experts agree that the design of the frame and suspension are important. They've also discovered that a lighter weight motorcycle is faster, more maneuverable, and easier to control.

A dirt bike sits high off the ground. That way it doesn't get damaged by big rocks, tree stumps, or bumps in the trail. The height of the bike keeps the engine safe. The chassis and most of the other parts of the bike are also made out of lightweight material. Keeping the weight down makes the motorcycle faster and easier to control.

Off-road motorcycles that are built to be street legal don't have to be as lightweight because they won't be raced over rough terrain. The main advantage for keeping the dual-purpose bikes as lightweight as possible is because a lighter motorcycle is easier to handle than a heavier bike.

Many parts on a dirt bike are different from the parts on street bikes. Dirt bike front forks are very high compared to the front forks on street bikes. A flexible plastic fender, or mud guard, sits high above the front tire. The handlebars sit at a comfortable height, not too high or too low. The rider needs to be comfortable enough to grip the bars for hours and sometimes days on end. Motocrossers sometimes attach hand protectors to the bars. A hand protector is the piece of plastic that sits in front of the driver's hand. Gravel or mud often flies onto the driver's hands and makes it hard for him or her to drive.

Some races require that a rider be on his bike for days at a time like this rider in the 1991 Paris-Dakar race.

The Parts of a Dirt Bike

Exhaust Pipe

Rear Fender

Rear Shocks

Seat

Gas Tank

Clutch Lever (Left Handlebar)

Throttle

Front Brake Lever

Handlebars

Front Forks

Front Shocks

Front Fender

Engine

Gear Shift Lever (Left Side)

Foot Peg

Chain

Rear Brake Pedal

Rear Wheel

Rear Tire

Chain Sprocket

Brake Line

Front Brake

Front Wheel

Front Tire

How a Two-Stroke Engine Works

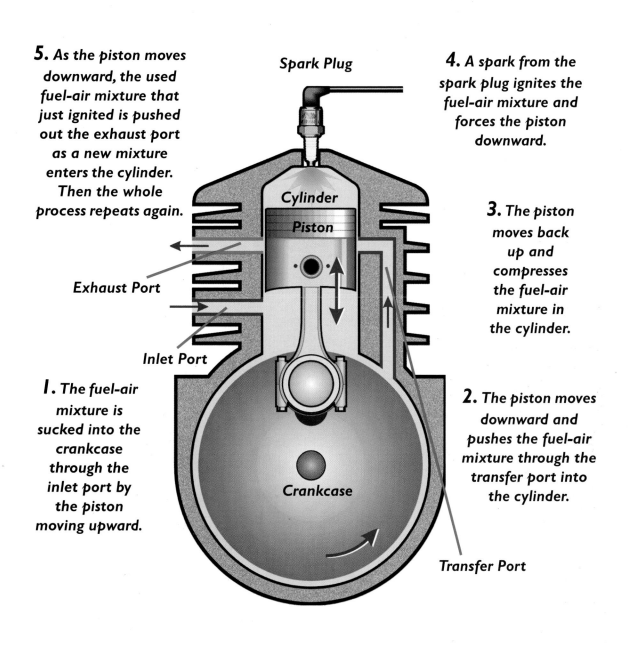

5. As the piston moves downward, the used fuel-air mixture that just ignited is pushed out the exhaust port as a new mixture enters the cylinder. Then the whole process repeats again.

4. A spark from the spark plug ignites the fuel-air mixture and forces the piston downward.

3. The piston moves back up and compresses the fuel-air mixture in the cylinder.

1. The fuel-air mixture is sucked into the crankcase through the inlet port by the piston moving upward.

2. The piston moves downward and pushes the fuel-air mixture through the transfer port into the cylinder.

Spark Plug

Cylinder

Piston

Exhaust Port

Inlet Port

Crankcase

Transfer Port

If the motorcycle is going to be driven on the street at all, it will need a headlight, taillight, turn signals, mirrors, a kick stand, and speedometer. These dual-purpose motorcycles are good for people who like to ride on both the street and the trail, but don't want two motorcycles. For a professional trail rider, a dual-purpose bike is too heavy and too slow. Professional trail bikes don't have any speedometers or mirrors. These things just get in the way and add more weight.

Long-travel suspension is used on most bikes built today. This type of suspension looks like a big spring attached from the swing-arm to the frame right below the seat. The seat is long so the rider can adjust his or her position when going up and down hills. A rider must adjust his or her weight on the bike in order to perform different maneuvers. The exhaust pipe usually sits below the seat on the bike so it doesn't get knocked around on rugged terrain.

The tires used on dirt bikes are called "knobbies." They are great for pushing a bike through sand and mud. Knobbies give the bike traction. On a paved street, those same knobby tires make for a bumpy ride. For the less serious trail rider who rides more on smooth, worn surfaces, a tire with less tread works better.

Opposite page: Most racing dirt bikes do not have mirrors, turn signals, or speedometers.

The Engine

The engine is the most important part of a dirt bike. When dirt bike racing first began in Europe, they used heavy four-stroke engines. When Americans started racing their bikes with two-stroke engines, they left Europeans far behind. The two-stroke engine is light weight. Most off-road motorcycles have this kind of engine.

There are four things that happen inside a cylinder: the intake of fuel, the compression of fuel, the explosion, and the exhaust. A four-stroke engine uses one stroke of a piston for each of these things. A two-stroke engine combines the intake and compression as a first stroke, and the explosion and exhaust as a second stroke.

The two-stroke engine is very powerful. The down sides of a two-stroke engine are that it runs hotter than a four-stroke engine, and it's dirtier. Oil is used to lubricate the piston, which moves up and down inside the cylinder. The engine burns a lot of oil compared to a four-stroke engine.

Just owning a fast bike with a big engine, however, won't assure you a win. You must also know how to drive skillfully, whether you are racing or just having fun.

Opposite page: Two-stroke engines are used in most dirt bikes.

Riding a Dirt Bike

Picking out a bike that fits you will make riding a lot easier. When you sit on the seat of the bike, make sure that your feet touch the ground easily. Don't get a bike that's too big for you or you won't be able to control it. Most people start out with an engine size of around 60 cc. As you get more skilled, you can buy a bigger motorcycle with a bigger engine.

Dirt bike riding takes a lot of skill. Whether riding for fun or professionally, there are some basic skills that all riders need. When first starting out, don't try to become a world-class trail rider. Take time and get comfortable with handling the bike and dealing with obstacles before trying any stunts.

Because trails are always bumpy and hilly, you need to learn to balance your weight on your feet while lifting yourself off the bike seat. Keep a relaxed but firm grip on the handle bars. Dirt trails will have sharp turns, steep hills, low gullies, loose gravel, mud, rivers, and unforeseen holes.

A rider has to always watch for objects in the path ahead. Being aware of what you're driving into is important, but it is also important to know how to handle these obstacles. Swerving around big rocks and knowing how to brake and stop quickly are important. Two very basic skills include going up and down hills.

Riding a dirt bike takes a lot of practice.

Going up hills can be tricky. Before climbing a hill, you need to build enough speed to reach the top. Going up a hill that is covered with loose dirt or sand can be hard if you give too little or too much throttle. Too much throttle will cause the rear wheel to spin and lose traction. Too little throttle won't push you up the hill at all.

If the hill is bumpy, raise yourself off the bike. Try to choose a straight path up the hill. If that isn't possible, just go full blast until you reach the top. If you don't get enough speed going and the trail is too difficult, turn around and go back down.

Going down hill takes control and balance. Choose your path carefully. Look for the straightest, smoothest path. If you come upon an obstacle, the best thing to do is slow down and go over it, or swerve around it. If the obstacle is too big to do either, just get off the bike and walk around it. Brake slowly and smoothly so you don't skid. Apply even pressure to both the front and rear brakes when going down a hill. When going down a hill controlling your speed is the most important thing.

Turning tight corners at high speeds can be dangerous. If you can't see around a corner, that means you can't see what's lying ahead on the road. There could be a fallen tree or loose gravel. People or animals could be in your path. Sometimes you can easily see the path ahead of you on a wide turn. If you want to

keep up speed around the turn, lean into the turn while turning up the throttle.

Driving across deep ruts, sand, and water can also create problems for the driver. Popping a wheelie is something that can be useful when going through water or over big ruts. A wheelie is the word used to describe the lifting of the front wheel off the ground and driving only on the back tire. It is very dangerous and requires a lot of control and skill. A stunt rider once rode for 38 arm-stretching miles (61 km) while popping a wheelie!

Riding down a hill takes a lot of control and balance.

To pop a wheelie, first shift your weight to the rear of the bike. Make sure you are balanced on the bike. Pull the clutch in all the way. Briefly crack the throttle wide open and let out the clutch while pulling (not too hard) on the handle bars. This should be done in first or second gear. Always keep both feet on the pegs.

While the tire is in the air, tap the rear brake lightly to bring the front tire down, or just let off the throttle. Practice these techniques under supervision and only after lots of time riding your trail bike. Practicing wheelies will teach you how to control your bike, and give you a good sense of balance.

Another good skill to learn is how to "spin a donut." Spinning a donut means to make a tight, sliding circle. The rider uses this technique to make a tight turn while maintaining motor speed.

To do this, drive in first gear while sliding your left foot along the ground. Slowly lean the motorcycle inward. Keep leaning on your left foot while giving the bike more gas. The back wheel will start to break loose and pivot. The front wheel will become more stationary as you give the engine more gas.

Making tight turns takes a lot of practice. You may fall a few times before getting it right, but it's a very helpful racing maneuver to know and master. It will get you around turns faster than your opponents.

These supercross racers are highly skilled riders.

Gear

Part of learning to ride a dirt bike is falling off your bike. With a little luck, and the right protective gear, dusting yourself off and jumping back on your motorcycle is all you'll have to do after a crash. Whether riding for fun, or for professional races, wearing the right gear is essential.

Full-face helmets offer the best protection. A helmet should feel snug and cover your mouth and chin. Always strap it on. A helmet doesn't do any good if it doesn't stay on your head. Goggles protect your eyes from flying dirt. When racing in a group, motorcycle tires can throw up a lot of rocks and gravel into the faces of those following close behind.

Long-sleeved shirts or jerseys protect you from getting scraped up if you fall. The brighter the color of the shirt the better, so other riders can see you. A chest protector, usually made out of plastic, will keep flying objects from injuring your chest.

Gloves give you a better grip on the handlebars. They are usually made out of nylon and leather. Serious trail riders wear pants that are made out of nylon with leather patches on the thighs and calves. Some even have plastic on the knees and thighs for extra protection. Boots, an important part of the dirt

bike rider's wardrobe, should be made out of leather and cover the whole foot and shin. The sole of the boot needs to be thick so it doesn't wear thin while being dragged over rugged terrain.

The basic idea of riding gear is to cover and support all of your body parts in case of an accident.

Safety

Wearing proper protective riding gear is important for safety, but following a few common sense rules will keep you from getting into big problems. Don't push yourself to try new maneuvers or stunts. Know your limits. Always ride with someone. Never go out alone. If you fall and hurt yourself, no one will know where you are and if you need help.

Make sure you know where you're going. Know how long you will be riding and gauge how far you are from home. Don't get caught in the dark. It's hardest to see at night, and it's risky to ride in the dark. Always stop when someone in your group stops. Don't ride away thinking they'll catch up. They may be in real trouble. Stay off of someone else's property. Get their permission first.

Before going for a ride, check your bike and make sure there's nothing wrong with it. Everyone should know how to maintain the most basic things on their bikes. In between rides, keep the bike clean. It's easier to see loose bolts and nuts when they're not covered in mud. Also, a leaky engine isn't noticeable when clumps of grass and sludge are plastered on the engine. Oiling the chain and changing the oil regularly are good ideas, too.

Before a ride, make sure the tires have enough air. The gas tank should be full. And it doesn't hurt to bring a compass and a few quarters for a pay phone in case you get lost. Always expect the unexpected to happen and use common sense. With those words of caution aside, learning to ride off road can be a life long experience.

Joining a trail-riding club can be a lot of fun. It's a good place to meet friends, and they usually have junior off-road races. There are many different kinds of off-road motorcycling. All of them promise not only the thrilling ride of the open trail, but also fun for a lifetime.

Always ride with someone else. Riding alone can be dangerous.

Glossary

Chassis - the frame of a motorcycle.

CC (Cubic Centimeters) - indicates the size of the engine. Technically, it is the size of the cylinder or area covered by the stroke of the piston.

Exhaust Pipe - the pipe that lets out the exhaust that comes from the engine.

Forks - a long pair of tubes that join the front wheel to the rest of the motorcycle. Inside are shock absorbers.

Four Stroke - a type of engine that uses four piston strokes, that uses an air intake and compression stroke as well as a power stroke.

Knobby Tires - tires that have small "knobs" sticking out of them. They are made for handling rugged terrain and giving good traction.

Long-Travel Suspension - a long, big spring that cushions a motorcycle.

Obstacle - something in the way.

Power Stroke - the stroke in a four-stroke engine in which the spark plug ignites the fuel mixture.

Speedometer - the dial showing the speed of the bike.

Terrain - the land.

Two-Stroke Engine - a type of engine that does not use valves to move gas inside the engine. It has a power stroke every second stroke of the piston.

Internet Sites

Minibike Central
http://www.geocities.com/MotorCity/7029/mini.html
This page shows pictures of awesome bikes and tells how to make them. It also has plenty of photos of minibikes and minicycles. This site will give you information on where to find minibikes and parts.

Pete's SOLO Disabled Motorcycle Project
http://www.btinternet.com/~chaloner/pete/pete.htm
This website is about a different kind of custom bike. The page is for disabled people who want to ride a motorcycle. See photos of this customized bike, and how it works.

The Dirt Bike Pages
http://www.off-road.com/orcmoto.html
This site has action photos of all kinds of dirt bikes, monthly columns and articles, and product reports. This site has important riding information, too.

Scooter Magazine Online
http://www2.scootermag.it/scooter/
This web site is fully devoted to motorscooters. Technique, developments, new models, tests, track and road trials.

The Motorcycle Database
http://www.motorcycle.informaat.nl/ehome.html
Over 250 motorcycles, their specifications and pictures, and driver experiences from visitors. Pick the model and year of motorcycle you would like to see. Photos and detailed information is included. Lots to see!

Pass It On

Motorcycle Enthusiasts: educate readers around the country by passing on information you've learned about motorcycles. Share your little-known facts and interesting stories. Tell others what your favorite kind of motorcycle is or what your favorite type of riding is. We want to hear from you!

To get posted on the ABDO & Daughters website E-mail us at
"Sports@abdopub.com"
Visit the ABDO Publishing Company website at www.abdopub.com

Index